Pundemonium
Vol. 1

James E. Larson

Lefse Press—Agoura Hills, Ca
ISBN: 979-8-9874392-0-3
eBook ISBN: 979-8-9874392-1-0
Title: *Pundemonium Vol. 1*
Author: James E. Larson
Digital distribution | 2022
Paperback | 2022

Dedication

The author dedicates this book to his loving family, wife Cindy, daughter Erica, and son Greg. They have had to listen to the author over the years trying out the various puns on them. They deserve recognition for enduring that pun-ishment.

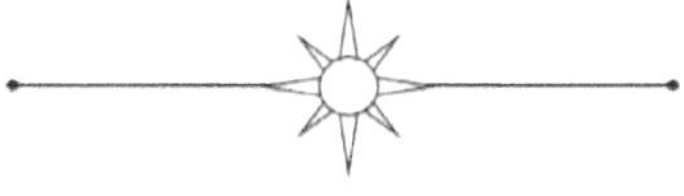

Chapter One

Did you hear about the chimney sweep got stuck in the fireplace chimney so long in the winter that when he got out he came down with the flue?

While cooking meat on the stove, the cook always had an upbeat message which was, "The bastings in life are free."

There was a dentist who joined the army because he wanted to be on their drill team.

Did you hear about the shepherd who continuously dreams about removing wool from sheep? It was a shear fantasy of his....

Did you hear about the financial investor who bought a mattress factory because he wanted to have something to fall back on?

There was a lazy animal trainer at the circus who was fired because he was seen lion down on the job.

I had heard once there was a medically trained fish that could operate on other fish...he was a sturgeon.

I know of a successful dermatologist who started from scratch...and never had to make a rash decision.

Two cannonballs had to get married...they ended up having BBs.

There is a new suntan location for pigs...it is called "Oikment!"

Two silk worms were in a race...they ended up in a tie.

A new orchestra musician was so confused he didn't know the difference between his brass and his oboe.

I know a baker so lazy he just loafed around all day....

I know an undertaker who had stiff competition with another funeral home....

Did you hear about the pedicurist that won a contest for the best looking hand at the salon where he worked...he nailed it.

The actor in the fish costume worked for scale.

The firefighter put out a small fire at the Synagogue with his hose... everybody yelled "Nozzletoff!"

There was a doctor who invented a home operating kit...it was called "Sutureself."

The baseball player at the plate accidentally hit a bird that flew by...he fowled it off....

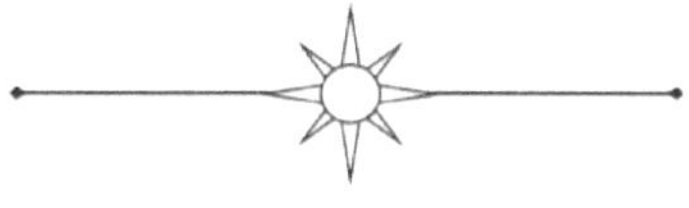

Chapter Two

They arrested a guy the other day that had a bowl of Jello in his jacket...they charged him with carrying a congealed weapon.

Some guy suggested a farmer raise ducks for a living...he said he would take a quack at it.

A rancher who raised deer and was trying to explain meaning of life to his teenage son said, "Son, you need to have doe to have fawn."

The marine biologist was arrested the other day for asking a fisherman to give him some free calamari in exchange for the biologist renting the fisherman's boat. The charge was "Squid pro Quo."

An elementary school teacher in Alaska asked her student, "Do we get fur from a skunk?"
  Little Johnny answered, "We get as fur as possible!"

I know an author who wrote a book about basements...he wanted to get on the best cellars list.

Two cowboys tied their horses so close together on the hitching rail that the two horses were fighting each other. The sheriff came by and gave a ticket to both cowboys for starting a "halter-cation."

The nurseryman underestimated the number of units he needed for a garden he was installing...he got caught with his plants down....

An Englishman opened a pub next to a nuclear reactor power plant...he called his pub "Fission and Chips."

The camper was very upset when the campground manager said he could not sleep in his camper...the camper still slept in the park but his anger was intents....

The lighting contractor put in low level lighting in the clients house by mistake...the homeowner took a dim view of that.

The fan dancer was arrested for stealing but she claimed her innocence...she said I have nothing to hide.

A former convict wanted to walk dogs for a living because he wanted a new leash on life....

When the Christmas tree lot operator allowed some people to cut down trees, he just realized he had opened up his first chopping center.

There was a sheikh who loved English type musicals so much he opened up a place where he sold his animals...it was called 'Camelot.'

Two horses were at a convention...one said to the other one, "I don't remember your mane but your pace is familiar."

The rancher sold some old saddles...then he threw in some extra saddle parts as he wanted to cinch the deal.

Chapter Three

The oilman, who seemed to swear all the time, offered to sell an oil well to a preacher...the preacher declined because it was a crude offer....

There was a man whose head was shaped just like a bullet...everybody kept saying to him, "A man of your caliper should go a long ways."

The candle lighter at the church said he only worked on wick ends.

The auto body shop had a sign out front that said, "May I Have The Next Dents?"

The seamstress, when asked how things were going, said, "Sew Sew."

The fireman, when offered a choice between working with a hose or something to climb up on, chose the latter.

A T V critic said, when he heard that a cow was going to host a T V show said, "That's udderly ridiculous."

A psychiatrist in California decided to start working with cows and analyze their problems...so far he only wants to work with cows who have a fodder complex.

The German undertaker, who always looks happy, also collected lots of funeral furniture. When asked why is he is so happy, he said, "Well, I always enjoy having a fine bier or two."

Two ranchers, who raised water fowl, had a bet that declared one rancher said that water fowl could live in a desert and the other rancher said that they could not...what they bet was a paradox.

Out in the old west, there was an Indian Chief called, "Chief Hock A Watch." ...he was a Pawnee.

Out in the old west there was a large Indian family that was always in a upbeat mood...said the father, "We just one big Hopi family."

A fisherman made a piano out of a large fish...when he had finished playing the scales he noticed the piano was out of tune. He said, "You know, you can tune a piano, but you can't tuna fish."

What do you get when you goose a ghost?...a handful of sheet.

A father names his daughter Carmen Cohen. The father had a habit of calling her either Carmen or Coen. By junior high school, she didn't know if she was Carmen or Coen.

The son of a farmer graduated from high school and he had excelled in all the horticultural classes, especially the part about the gathering the reproductive parts of the plants...he was voted most likely to sack seed.

Chapter Four

Two woman race car drivers got into fight over a certain purse...in the fight, they damaged one of their cars. The auto body manager labeled the damage as a Fendi bender.

The truck driver only worked part time...he was semi-retired.

Little known fact: Alexander Graham Bell's real name was Alexander Graham Bell Poloski...he was the first telephone pole.

A guy who supplied small amphibious creatures to the high school science classes had his delivery van parked in a no parking zone...the policeman had no choice but to have him toad away.

The bootlegger moonlighted as a song writer...in fact one of his first hits was, "In the Still of the Night."

The little boy accidentally ate the worm of a fisherman's hook. The rest of the day he spoke with baited breath....

The mayor of a small town wanted a local chicken rancher to run for office. The rancher first said no, but the mayor kept egging him on....

The manager of the tall tower in Pisa Italy was accepting bids from contractors who said they could straighten the tower...the manager hasn't hired any contractor yet, but he was leaning toward one....

Two Xmas tree salesman had a bet who could sell the most trees. The loser eventually boughed out.

The love lorn advice columnist was advising a reader who just could not get this man to be interested in her. The columnist said, "If at first you don't succeed, try a little ardor."

The heating and air conditioning contractor was so neat, he always tried to keep his ducts in a row....

It is no wonder that many dentists are sad...they are always caught looking down in the mouth....

There was a reporter that put a story in the newspaper about an incident that included a group of old fishermen in a smoke shop sitting around a tobacco oriental water pipe that was also filled with citrus water and a skunk that came in the back door and caused everybody to flee. It seemed that story was a hoax. The reporter was laughing because he said some people fell for everything in that story hookah, lime, and stinker...

The weather forecasting warned his audience that it was going to rain cats and dogs today...he said be careful and don't step in a poodle....

There was an old butcher shop in the Bronx that just got robbed. The owner said, "I guess we are going to have to beef up security."

There was an old Indian Chief who was going bald, so he bought a wig. He said he liked to apply heat to the hairpiece before he went out in the snow...he said he always liked to keep his wig warm....

Chapter Five

The bricklayer, who just arrived at the job site, witnessed a very bad accident. A brick wall he was working on blew up... he was totally mortar-fied.

The military arms expert had a accident with one of his weapons in his collection...it went off without warning leaving him mortar-fied.

There once was a strange musician who made a xylophone out of several fish laid side by side. He would hit the fish on the area where they used to breathe. He would exclaim, "The gills are alive with the sound of music!"

There was a young man who was set to inherit a lot of money, but he unfortunately got run over by a steamroller. This was the first example of compressed heir....

In England, there is an ale called Ann Boleyn Beer...it does not have a head on it....

A real estate agent was trying to decide whether or not to try to sell a houseboat on the river even though the houseboat was not level and it was lower on one side than the other. In the end, the agent decided to take the listing anyway....

A man broke in to a Sea World amusement park and tried to write graffiti on one of the aquatic mammals. He was arrested and the judge sentenced him to 90 days because he did it on porpoise....

An old bald man ordered a very expensive hair piece. When he got it he refused to send the company any money. The case went to court and the judge said because he took possession of the hair piece, he had toupee.

A delicatessen owner was having a sale on some food he wanted to get rid off...they were some Jewish salmon, some chicken soup broth, and a plain bun. Some person bought everything, Lox, stock, and bare roll.

It is said melon pickers can marry but they cantaloupe.

The rink owner was losing money every day...he said he was just skating by.

A rug cleaning business wanted to increase their business. They went to a marketing company. When they found out how much it would cost to use their services, they were floored.

On the Discovery Channel, the people on the show Gold Rush had a saying, "At a location, if Gold we stay, Ore we don't."

A duck went into a drug store and asked the clerk, "I would like to buy some Chap stick."
   The clerk said, "Do you want to pay for it now?"
   "No," said the duck, "just put it on my bill."

A bridge designer was asked, what is the most important part of a bridge that you honor...the bridge designer said, "Well, I was always taught to respect your piers."

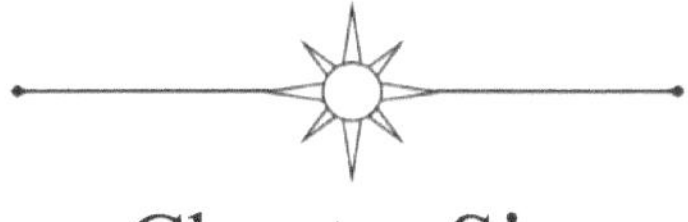

Chapter Six

On a cake show on T V the contestants were instructed to make a cake in the shape of their favorite baseball player...when it was time to start, the announcer said, "Batter Up!"

In Tibet, a farmer rode a wild ox all day in the hot sun. Somehow at the end of the day the ox got to close to the campfire and the ox caught fire. The farmer, dealing with his aches and pains, grabbed a pail of water and said... "Oh my baking Yak."

A bartender I know made a new kind of drink the other day. He mixed "Milk of Magnesia" with vodka. He called it a 'Phillips Screwdriver.'

The new intern at the Heinz factory just started working in the tomato division...he had a long way to ketchup....

A little known fact: Some Minute Men cooks in the Revolutionary War trained some chickens to find wherever the British soldiers were hiding. This was the cooks first case of 'Chicken catch a Tory.'

Two golfers in Mexico played in a golf tournament and each thought that they had won...the argument got so heated that Jamie shot Juan...at least at the end of the day, Jamie could claim he shot a hole in Juan...

In a Las Vegas showroom, a juggler's act consists of him juggling very large knives. The critics say his act is on the cutting edge.

A clothing store's monthly income was noticeably down at this time of year because this was their slack season.

A new owner of a bakery had a policy where the bakers could make one loaf of bread a day for themselves. The owner wanted to give them what they kneaded.

Hard to believe, but some rancher in Texas trained a pony to sing a little. However, before the first concert, the pony got a sore throat and they had to cancel the concert. After all, he was a little hoarse.

In the old west, a bank robber got dressed up in woman's clothes and then proceeded to rob a bank. It took a while for the posse to get underway, but when they did they came upon the robber's old campfire.
    After looking around, a deputy held up a piece of woman's clothing and said, "Looks like he gave us the slip."

There was a narcissistic woman who was running a blood bank. She was a very vein person.

The seamstress had so many skirts to shorten that she was starting to feel hemmed in....

The mother of a future German composer always made sure her son had something with him at elementary school to eat for the noon meal. Actually, this became the first example of a Bach's lunch.

A vocal teacher was wondering if her student could sing his part in the local production of The Messiah. When asked, the student replied, "I think I can Handel it."

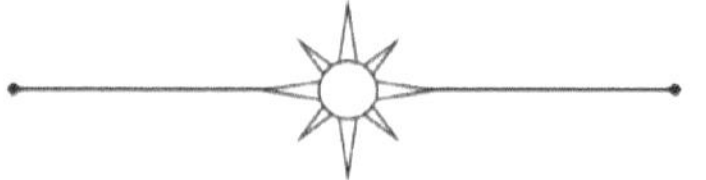

Chapter Seven

Why can't a steam engine set down? Because it has a tender behind.

Two people met at the Liberty Bell exhibit in Philadelphia. One said, "I am Mr. Richards."

The other guy said, "I am Mr. Clapper."

Mr. Richards said, "I think I know you from somewhere...I don't remember your face, but your name rings a bell."

In Yellowstone National Park, it is the law that every 200 years, buffalo lovers can gather together and celebrate their Bison- tennial.

Years ago, there were a group of people who learned how to write letters using their feet. Today, that story is just a footnote in history....

It is true that relatives who get together to make a lot of things from yarn become a very close knit family.

When a animal trainer decided to only train large water mammals, the trainers fate was sealed....

A circus in Europe advertised that one of its acts was a large 400 pound Czechoslovakian acrobat doing his routine on a trampoline. He was billed as the world's largest bouncing Czech....

In the old west, a wild underage ranch hand road up to the saloon and walked up to the door. The bouncer would not let him in. The ranch hand got back in his saddle and just then, the parts of the saddle where he puts his boots fell off. He got so mad, he threw them at the saloon window and the window broke. The people around him said he just wanted to stirrup something...

A minor league baseball player in Seattle seamed to play his absolute best right after every rainstorm.
The team named him MVP...Moist Valuable Player.

Whenever Medusa went to visit her local beauty parlor, the staff would recoil in horror...and then become stoned....

A barber experimented with adding lacquer to the old man's sparse hair to make it look fuller and shinier...when the barber came back a half hour later to see the results, the lacquer had varnished into thin hair....

The old man who had worked in a cheese factory was teaching a new hire how to separate the layer of cream from milk which was in a very large container. The new employee did not follow the old man's directions.
    The new employee said, "There's got to be more than one way to skim a vat!"

The cowboy shoe salesman had a habit of never charging for socks when he sold his shoes...he always threw them in to boot.

If you want to be polite in somebody's house when you notice a strange odor, just ask them if they are aware their house has "House-itosis."

Chapter Eight

When the young Dutch boy brought some cheese to his class's Show and Tell, his teacher gave him a wonderful grade because it was all Gouda!

When the long-winded Congressman wound up his concise and forcefully expressive speech, he ran to the restroom as he was feeling kind of pithy....

The old bricklayer mason was so tired of working such long hours, he decided to throw in the trowel....

A battery salesperson kept reading up on sales brochures about all the new batteries. He wanted to keep current.

The furniture maker, who was adding coloring to the chair he just made, did not like how it turned out...he looked at the chair he had just worked on with disdain.

Before the convention, the fisherman thought it would be fun to have some fish he caught imprinted with his boat charter business name and phone number. He spent a lot of time at the convention saying, "Hello, I would like to give you my cod."

The slow working butcher was working in his shop which was very hot inside...he only had a large fan right behind him. Every time he bent over to help a customer, he got a little behind on the order....

The doctor was feeling down about the fact that his office waiting room did not have anybody in it. The short tempered doctor yelled about that because he didn't have any patients.

A wealthy person invited a bunch of neighborhood boys on his yacht. The boys got into a fight at the rear of the boat so the owner of the boat went to the rear of the boat and gave the boys a stern warning.

A little known fact, the big corporation that makes Clorox once had a singing group they sponsored. The singing group was known as "The Bleach Boys."

The bread maker's assistant only wanted to work on the part of the bread making that added the element that makes the bread rise...he said it was the yeast he could do.

The old professional baseball player, had a strange collection of pets. His favorite one was a pet bat who just died. He had given eulogies for other pets before, but he started to cry when he was talking about this pet. It was said he must have just been following old baseball rules as when he started playing baseball years ago, as he was always told to "choke up on the bat."

When Jesus was born, it was a manger event.

The old Norwegian said he invented a game called 'Lutefisk' but he said it never cod on.

The old fisherman was making a pickled small fish with some vinegar. Somehow, by accident, some of the solution got in his ear. He soon became hard of herring.

A college botany professor gave his students a quiz on naming a certain part of a flower. He was such a good teacher that all the students came up with the right anther.

Chapter Nine

A podiatrist wrote a bestselling book. It was filled with a lot of foot notes.

A tree trimmer I know wanted to open up a branch office.

A surfer in Malibu was making a model of a dolphin out of seaweed, but thought the sculpture was missing something. So he asked his friend if he could give him some kelp....

The unhappy employee at the pillow factory, who was in charge of filling the pillows, was feeling down.

A geology professor in a small university in Colorado was telling his students about a certain favorite rock formation. He said if they did not label it correctly on the upcoming test, they shale not pass...

A guy from Seattle ran a marathon race in a hot dog costume and he won. The reporter asked him how does it feel to be a weiner?

A baking company found out one of their employees was really good at karate. So they asked him to help the company sponsor a karate tournament. It seems the company had found their own "dough-jo."

In Australia, a sheep herder rode his animals in a sheep only rodeo. The authorities said he owed a lot of money to many people. They tried to catch him but he was always on the lamb.

A farmer in South Dakota trained a young female chicken to type on a word processor. Sometime a sentence would be produced. The farmer put all the sentences in a book and published it. Surprisingly, it won a "Pulletzer Prize."

The young female calf was romping around in the pasture...her display was a true example of "Heifer-vescence."

Dumbo, the flying pachyderm, was okay with people asking him how does he fly. He did not like it when they asked him why does he fly...it thought that question was irrelephant.

The plumber was having trouble with fixing a leak...he was having a bad day at the orifice....

About the Author

The author, James E. Larson, has always enjoyed a good pun. Just recently, he decided to create new ones for a book. He says like anything else, some puns come easy while other need some rewrites before they are finished. A good pun needs a good back story that sets up the 'Pun-ch Line.' That is the fun part of creating puns.